AMELIA EARHART

The Absolutely Untrue, Totally Made Up,
100% Fake Life Story
of a Great American Aviator

by Alan Katz
illustrations by TRACY HILL

Tanglewood • Indianapolis

Published by Tanglewood Publishing, Inc.
Text © 2020 Alan Katz
Illustrations © 2020 Tracy Hill

Cover and Interior art by Tracy Hill
Design by Amy Alick Perich

Tanglewood Publishing, Inc.
1060 N. Capitol Ave., Ste. E-395
Indianapolis, IN 46204
www.tanglewoodbooks.com

Printed in the USA by Lake Book Manufacturing.
10 9 8 7 6 5 4 3 2 1

ISBN 978-1-939100-48-1

Library of Congress Control Number: 2020940161

Dedication:

To Amelia Earhart,
who inspired so many
by soaring so high

One

On her first birthday, Amelia Earhart dedicated her life to flight.

"Aga boo ka pleh ma," is what the adults standing near her heard.

"Isn't that cute?" asked her mother.

"It's totally adorable," answered her father.

"Sheer poetry!" exclaimed her grandparents at the exact same time. Then they both said, "Jinx. You owe me a soda! Jinx. You owe me a soda!" over and over.

But Amelia hadn't said anything cute, adorable, or poetic. According to the exact translation in the Larry Webster Baby-to-

English Dictionary, what Amelia had said was...

"I believe that I will dedicate my life to flight. I believe that there is a way for women and men to soar high above the clouds to places as yet unreached. I believe I can make a powerful difference in this world. And most of all, at this very moment, I believe that I need a diaper change."

Later that day, Amelia's grandmother won $1,000 in the lottery. And her grandfather tripped over a footstool and broke his nose (fortunately, the footstool wasn't damaged). But those events were not really important to Amelia's life story. Or were they? By the time you finish this book, you'll know.

Let's fast-forward a year or two—which is something you really can't do in real life, no matter how expensive a remote control you buy. In other words, let's jump to Amelia Earhart's third birthday.

Two

Welcome to Amelia Earhart's third birthday party. Please don't pop the balloons. Please don't eat the food or stick your fingers in the cake.

Why didn't you bring a gift?

Much like Amelia's second birthday party, this was a noisy, noisy event filled with crabby, crabby people. The parents were busy yelling at the kids, and the kids were busy yelling at each other. No one was having any fun. And then...

Amelia stood on the couch and said, "Look at me, soaring high above the clouds! I am flyinging!"

"Wowie, wowie, wow," said all the kids.

"Amelia Earhart, get off that couch!" her mother said. "And also, there's no such word as 'flyinging.' You mean flying."

Amelia listened to her mother and jumped off the couch, yelling, "Look at me! I'm landinging!"

"You mean 'landing,'" her mother insisted. "Not landinging."

Being corrected twice in a row at her own birthday party was too much for Amelia. She immediately started sobbinging.

No one knew what to do. Then her next-door neighbor, Franklin David Peppermouth, had a good idea: "Hey Amelia, you should open the gifts," he said.

"Great idea, Franklin!" Amelia brightened. "But you weren't invited to this party, I don't know how you got in here, and you really should go home."

"Oh," said Franklin as he walked out.

Amelia smiled and laughed and cheered as she opened present after present. Her mother had told all the gift-givers how much Amelia liked airplanes, so everyone gave her something to do with flight.

She got a fancy plane.

A plain plane.

A fancy plane used by farmers to drop grain.

Also a plain grain plane.

A plain grain plane made in Maine (from Wayne).

The same plain grain plane made in Maine (from Jane).

And her favorite gift of all: One-hundred tiny bags of stale peanuts that she'd someday be able to give out when she was a real aviator with a real plane and real passengers.

See, that was Amelia's dream. And no one, absolutely no one, could stop Amelia when she was dreaminging.

Three

Sometime during Amelia's year in fourth grade, her mother took her for a hearing test. The test proved that Amelia's hearing was fine.

The next year, her mother took her for a vision test. The test proved that Amelia's vision was fine.

And one year later, her mother took her for a dental exam. The exam proved that Amelia's teeth were fine.

In fact, they were better than fine.

"Yes indeedy, you've got the most beautiful teeth within 62.6 miles," her dentist, Dr. Young, told her that day. "In fact, I'd like to

remove all of your teeth so I can show my other patients just how well you've taken care of them."

"No!" said Amelia.

"Please?" begged her dentist. "After all, there are so many kids who don't practice proper dental hygiene, and if I could just show them how white and healthy your teeth are, I know they'd want to do a better job on theirs."

"Absolutely not," said Amelia.

"I'd be happy to hang them on the wall in a showcase, with a sign that says, *Just look at how well Amelia Earhart takes care of her teeth.*

"If you displayed all my teeth, what would I do at mealtime?" the girl wanted to know.

"Have soup," the dentist replied. "Soup is yummy."

"I can't have soup at every meal!" Amelia said.

"Of course not," the dentist told her. "But there are plenty of other chew-less foods you can enjoy, like pudding, gelatin, and cotton candy..." he told her.

"But cotton candy is so sugary, it's bad for my teeth!" Amelia exclaimed.

"Not if they're hanging on my wall!" the doctor insisted.

"Forget it!" Amelia blurted out as she jumped out of the chair.

"It's not for me, Amelia. Just think of little Timmy Borden, who has an appointment later today. He always shows up with rotten, smelly teeth and disgusting, oozing gums that are so horrible that I can't even talk about them—even though I pretty much just did."

"It's out of the question," Amelia insisted.

"I am leaving here with my perfectly wonderful teeth."

"All of them?" the dentist wanted to know.

"All of them."

"Okay," the dentist sighed. "I'll see you in six months."

"Thank you," said Amelia, deep down knowing she probably had to look for a new dentist.

Four

"I am now going to write on the board all about the miracle of man being able to soar in an airplane," Amelia Earhart's fifth-grade teacher announced early one morning.

Amelia couldn't contain her excitement. And although she was usually a perfectly well-behaved student, upon hearing what her teacher said, Amelia shouted out, "Within ten years, *I* am going to do that!"

The kids laughed at the rather loud interruption. They laughed even more when the teacher smiled and told Amelia, "Young lady, I believe that is something you can do right now. Today. There is simply no reason for you to wait ten years!"

"Why thank you, Mrs. Borden!" Amelia yelled to her teacher, who was a wonderful, wonderful educator though not so terrific when it came to taking care of her son's teeth. But that was another matter.

Amelia immediately ran to the clothes closet and took out a large suitcase. Then she opened it and pulled out an aviator's helmet, an aviator's scarf, an aviator's jacket, and some printed flyers about the upcoming Spring Carnival. She stuffed the flyers back into the bag and quickly put on the helmet, scarf, and jacket.

"Okay, Mrs. Borden, I'm ready for my first solo flight—where's the plane?" Amelia wanted to know.

The class was laughing harder than ever.

"Whatever do you mean, Amelia?" Mrs. Borden asked her.

"You said you're going to write on the board about the miracle of flying in an airplane. I said I planned to do that within 10 years, and you said it was something I could do right now. So can I?"

"Amelia, dear," the teacher said softly. "I thought you meant you someday planned to write on the board. I said you could do that

now. Which you can, little one; here's the
chalk."

The class started laughing so loudly that
many of the students were literally rolling
on the floor. In fact, Amelia had to step over
Ben Daniels so she could take the chalk and
write on the board:

And with that, Amelia returned to her
seat and gritted her teeth, which she was
mighty glad were still in her mouth.

Five

Today at 5 p.m.! Right here! Come see the amazing stunt pilot Bob Johnson!, the sign said in big letters. Amelia couldn't believe her eyes. Imagine...a real stunt pilot coming to her little town!

She stepped up to the sign to read what it also said, in much smaller print:

This sign was created by Nelson Brothers Sign Makers, creators of fine signs for homes, schools, businesses, and county fairs. If you need a sign, just stop by between the hours of 9 a.m. and 5 p.m., Monday through Friday, though please don't come between 1 p.m. and 2 p.m., because that's when Larry

Nelson goes to lunch, Howard Nelson takes a nap, and Nelson Nelson goes to the bank (if there's any money to deposit). Of course, Ernie Nelson will be there between 1:00 p.m. and 2:00 p.m., but he has terrible handwriting, and if you order a sign from him and you want it to say, Sale on Suits, *when he's done, it might look more like* Safe or Sodas, *which doesn't actually mean anything. And if you don't believe us, just ask Ed and Susan Smith, who recently had to hang one of Ernie's signs that seemed to say,* Gappy Terthday, Umple Frep!

Amelia stopped reading the message there, because it seemed a little silly to her. But she went back to the big lettering on the top and said to herself, "Wow, I'm gonna see a stunt pilot!"

Amelia looked at her watch, which had little wings instead of hands on it. The little wing was on the four, and the big wing was on the six, which meant it was 4:30. Only thirty minutes until the stunt pilot! Amelia sat down in the field and waited. And waited. And waited. About an hour later, a man came to remove the sign.

"What are you doing?" asked Amelia.

"Removing the sign," the man said.

"B-b-b-but why?" she asked.

"Because the stunt pilot was here yesterday!" the man told her.

"Yesterday? What? The sign says *today!*" Amelia insisted.

"On the top, it does," the man agreed. "But waaaaay down here on the bottom, right after it says, *Gappy Terthday, Umple Frep!*, it says, *Sorry Amelia Earhart, you're here a day late.*

"I didn't read that far down," Amelia whined.

"No one ever does," said the man. "No one ever does."

Amelia watched as the man walked away with the sign. The farther away he got, the smaller he looked. And just before he was totally out of sight, he turned around and yelled back to Amelia, "No one ever does."

"WHAT?" she called.

"No one ever does," he shouted.

"Oh," said Amelia, as she wrote in the dirt with a stick:

Six

"Grandma," Amelia said one night at the dinner table. "May I ask you three questions?"

"Certainly," her grandmother replied.

"First, I'd like to ask if you would use the $1,000 you won in the lottery in Chapter One to buy me my very own airplane."

Her grandmother sliced a piece of baked chicken, gently put it into her mouth, and stared at Amelia for what seemed like an hour. When she'd finally finished chewing, she smiled a broad smile at Amelia and said, "What?"

"I'd like to ask if you would use the $1,000 you won in the lottery in Chapter

One to buy me my very own airplane,"
Amelia repeated.

"And what's the third question?" her
grandmother wanted to know.

"Third question?" Amelia said. "That's
my first question!"

"But you asked it twice, so it counts
twice," her grandmother insisted.

"I don't think so!" Amelia responded.

"Listen, you're lucky I didn't count,
Grandma, may I ask you three questions?
as your first question!" the wise old lady
said.

"Grandma, are you serious?" Amelia said.

"And that could be the third! All done!"

Grandmother exclaimed as she smiled and spit out some of the baked chicken bones.

"Grandma, that's unfair! You can't count the first question twice, or the question to ask if I could ask questions *at all*," Amelia protested.

"Okay fine, I won't count the question to ask if you could ask questions as a question," Amelia's grandmother said. "Now then, the answer to the first question is no, I will not use the $1,000 I won in the lottery in Chapter One to buy you your very own airplane."

"Awww!" Amelia said.

"The answer to your second question, also about using the $1,000 I won in the lottery in Chapter One to buy you your very own airplane, is no."

"Awwwwwwwwww!" Amelia said.

"Now what's your third question?" Amelia's grandmother inquired.

Feeling defeated, Amelia made a very simple request. "May I have an extra portion of applesauce tonight, Grandma?" she asked.

"Why yes, sweetie, of course," her grandmother replied.

"Thank you, Grandmother," Amelia said as she used her fork to scratch a message into the chicken gravy on her plate:

Seven

Up to this point in the story, Amelia seems to be a little girl who faced a lot of disappointment. But the truth is, she was a pretty happy person. She went to dances. She sang in the school choir. She had many friends, got good grades, and was known to be helpful, responsible, and kind.

And yet every night as her head hit the pillow, she could think of nothing but flight. She imagined herself being able to leave the ground and fly high above her house, waving to her grandmother, giving a thumbs-up to all the neighbors, and feeling the freedom of soaring up among the clouds.

That was her dream. That was her goal. And on a special, special, special day in June of her 17th year, that dream and goal came true. Sort of.

It was 1:05 p.m., and Amelia heard a loud rapping on the door. She put down the remote control (which was useless anyway, because there was nothing to remotely control) and ran to the door to find...

Nelson Nelson.

The sign maker, Nelson Nelson, was breathless as he excitedly told Amelia,

"Man, fly, sky, hit, lot!"

"Ear, dog, lip, zoo, gum, wet!" Amelia shouted back, thinking they were playing some kind of game where they had to call out unrelated three-letter words.

By that time, Nelson Nelson had caught his breath and was able to tell her, "Young lady, listen, a man was flying an airplane in the sky. The plane came down and hit a lot of cornstalks before coming to a stop in a parking lot!"

"What? Man, fly, sky, hit, lot?" Amelia asked.

"Yes!" he told her.

"Let's go!" said Amelia (who fortunately had not taken off her helmet, scarf, or flying jacket since that fifth-grade blackboard incident).

Within minutes, Nelson Nelson and Amelia were on the scene. A plane had indeed come down and skidded to a stop in the Shop Cheap Here Now parking lot! Amelia saw that there was absolutely no damage to the plane, and watched with great interest as the pilot hopped out of the plane, threw down his helmet, and said, "My wife was right! I don't know how to fly that thing! From now on I'm keeping both feet on the ground and sticking to being a dentist, even if Timmy Borden's teeth do make me sick!"

"Dr. Young?" Amelia exclaimed. "Is that your plane?"

"Not anymore!" the dentist said. "I've given up flying for good! By the way, are you still brushing and flossing regularly?"

"Yes, I am," said Amelia proudly.

"I am, too," said Nelson Nelson, though no one was listening to him.

"Amelia, even though you wouldn't give me your teeth, I'm still proud of you," Dr. Young said.

"Are you proud of me, too?" asked Nelson Nelson, though no one was listening to him.

Amelia had a thought. "Dr. Young," she said. "May I ask you three questions?"

"Of course, Amelia," he said as he dusted himself off.

"First, may I have this plane?"

"Yes," said the dentist.

Amelia never even had to ask the second and third questions (or just the third, depending on whether or not you believed her grandmother that in situations like that, *May I ask you three questions?* counts as the first).

Eight

Raise your hand if you've ever been on an airplane. No, the other hand. Okay, you can put it down now.

If you've been on a plane, then you know the exciting feeling Amelia Earhart had the day she jumped behind the controls of the plane Dr. Young had just given her.

"Golly!" Amelia exclaimed as she sat there as Nelson Nelson pushed the airplane back to her house.

"Thanks, Mister!" Amelia said once they reached her front door. "I can't pay you, but believe me, anytime you want to go flying, you just come back here and I'll take you up in this amazing plane."

"You're dreaming, kid," Nelson Nelson said. "Girls can't fly planes! That's a job for men, though apparently not for dentists."

(Nelson Nelson was wrong about everything he'd said—girls and women *can* fly planes, and so can dentists. According to the Federal Board of Dental Aviators, many, many dentists fly their own planes. Recent slightly inaccurate studies show that dentists rank third among all medical professionals as aviators; only foot doctors and shoulder surgeons fly more.)

Amelia didn't know all that. All she knew was he was wrong about girls not being able to fly planes. And she would prove him wrong. Oh boy, would she prove him wrong. Wrong, wrong, wrong, wrong, wrong. WRONG!

"You're wrong about girls not being able to fly planes," Amelia said. "And I will prove you wrong. Oh boy, will I prove you wrong. Wrong, wrong, wrong, wrong, wrong. WRONG!"

"Oh yeah?" Nelson Nelson said. "How?"

"Girls and women *can* fly planes, and so can dentists. According to the Federal

Board of Dental Aviators, many, many dentists fly their own planes. Why, recent slightly inaccurate studies show that dentists rank third among all medical professionals as aviators; only ear doctors and liver surgeons fly more."

"I thought it was only foot doctors and shoulder surgeons that fly more," Nelson Nelson said.

"Yes, that was true on page 30. But even *more recent* slightly inaccurate studies show it's changed since then," Amelia told him.

"I believe you, and I'm very sorry I said that girls can't fly planes," Nelson Nelson said.

"Thank you," replied Amelia. "And I also think you should apologize to dentists, foot doctors, shoulder surgeons, ear doctors, and liver surgeons."

"I will, next time I meet some," Nelson Nelson said.

"I'm a dentist!" said a man who just happened to be wandering by.

"I'm a foot doctor!" said another man who just happened to be wandering by.

"I'm an ear doctor!" said a third man who just happened to be wandering by.

"I'm a professional field goal kicker!" said a fourth man who just happened to be wandering by. "But my wife is a liver surgeon, and I can accept an apology on her behalf."

"I'm sorry to all of you," Nelson Nelson said.

"Thank you," the first three men said.

"I'll tell my wife," said the fourth man.

"Thank you," said Nelson Nelson.

Then they all went home.

Nine

Amelia Earhart so loved reading that she read over two thousand books in her lifetime. But no matter what she was reading, she always, always skipped Chapter Nine. And that's what she'd want you to do, too. So let's move on to Chapter Ten, in which you'll find everything that you were supposed to read in Chapter Nine.

By the way, when you're reading any book other this one, skipping Chapter Nine is a lousy idea. Very often, Chapter Nine is the one in which they tell you who stole the diamonds, or who broke Aunt Selma's vase, or who stepped on Nathan's peanut butter and jelly sandwich and caused a terrible purple and brown stain on the rug at Mrs. Simone's Haircutting Salon and Taco Shop.

In other words, it's never a good idea to skip Chapter Nine. Except perhaps in this book.

But come to think of it, it's a little late to do that.

So let's move on to Chapter Ten. And please don't step on Nathan's peanut butter and jelly sandwich as you turn the page (or else you might end up in Chapter Nine of a book called *Who Stepped on Nathan's Peanut Butter and Jelly Sandwich?*).

Ten

It was a crisp and clear morning. The sun was shining. There wasn't a single cloud in the sky. The wind was calm.

"Amelia Earhart," Amelia Earhart said to Amelia Earhart. "Today is someday."

"No it's not, it's Saturday," said a man in a blue raincoat standing alongside a duck. "Tomorrow is someday."

Curiously, the duck agreed.

"No sir, no duck," said Amelia. "Today is the someday that I fly. Today I soar, up there into the sky!"

"You're going to need a plane," the man said.

"I have one!" exclaimed Amelia.

"You're going to need pilot's gear," the man said.

"I have it!" exclaimed Amelia.

"You're going to need special training," the man said.

"I have it. I took an online course on the Internet this morning!" exclaimed Amelia.

The man had no idea what she meant by "online" or "Internet," but he recognized the words "this morning," so he gave Amelia a thumbs-up.

"Then good luck, little lady," he said as he patted her on the back.

Curiously, the duck also gave her a thumbs-up. He also handed her his lucky banana peel.

"Well, I'm off!" beamed Amelia, waving to them as she got into her plane.

"I'll say she's off...*she's off her rocker!*" the man said to his duck.

"Hey, you're the one talking to a duck," said the duck. "So maybe *she's* not the crazy one."

"Good point," said the man.

"I hope I get my lucky banana peel back," said the duck as he unluckily fell into a hole in the ground and broke his binoculars.

Eleven

Amelia Earhart sat in the cockpit and took a deep breath.

"This is the moment you've been waiting for your whole life, Amelia," Amelia told herself. "Let's soar," she said to the airplane, declaring it her *VEHICLE OF MAGICAL INTERNATIONAL TRAVEL.*

Amelia didn't realize that the initials of what she called the plane spelled out V.O.M.I.T. She was simply too excited.

Amelia checked the big dial with the needle-looking thing on it. She checked the smaller dial with the double-needle-looking thing on it. She checked the wind doohickey. (Listen, she checked everything there was to check, and *she* knew exactly what they all meant, but since *she's* the aviator and you're not and I'm not, let's not get technical here.)

"All systems go!" Amelia shouted as she put her foot on the thing you're supposed to put your foot on.

The plane wiggled. It jiggled. It sputtered. It puttered. Some might say it muttered. And then...

It rolled. Forward. Fast. Faster. Faster. Faster. Faster. And then...

IT TOOK OFF!

IT ACTUALLY TOOK OFF!

IN THE AIR!

UP IN THE SKY!

Ten feet! Then twenty! Thirty! Forty-six and-a-half! Thirty-seven-and-fifteen-sixteenths! Ninety!

"That's one small step for a girl named Amelia Earhart," Amelia said. "And one giant leap for a girl named Amelia Earhart."

Amelia liked the sound of that. It struck her both as poetic and historic. So she said it again, over and over, until...

The plane went splerk! Blerk! Gerk! And then, luckily for Amelia, it floated slowly back to earth, softly returning Amelia to the exact spot where she'd started!

"Wow, that was one soft landing for a girl named Amelia Earhart," Amelia said. "And, um, er, one soft landing for a girl named Amelia Earhart."

Amelia knew that statement wasn't poetic *or* historic. But she liked the sound of it, and she *loved* the flight!

Twelve

"Mother, I'm home!" the extremely happy girl called as she stepped into the house after her amazing flight.

"Amelia Earhart," her mother bellowed from the next room. "I told you not to step one foot off our block—I hope you didn't disobey me!"

"I didn't, mother!" Amelia said, smiling to herself. "I didn't step one foot off our block, I promise!"

Technically, Amelia was telling the truth.

She'd *flown* miles away but hadn't actually *stepped* off her block.

"That's a good girl," her mother said.

"Although I do wonder why you're smiling to yourself, little lady."

"I'm smiling to myself because today is someday!" Amelia said.

"No it's not, it's Saturday," her mother replied, not realizing that the same joke had already been made in Chapter Ten. "My dear, today it seems as if you've got your head in the clouds!"

"Almost," Amelia said, smiling to herself.

"There you go, smiling to yourself again," Amelia's mother scowled. "What's that for?"

"Don't you want your daughter to be happy, mother?" Amelia asked.

"Of course I do, sweetie," her mother replied.

"Well, I am, mother," Amelia said.

"That's all I want in life," her mother told her, smiling to herself.

"Why are you smiling to yourself, mother?" Amelia wanted to know.

"No reason," said her mother—although there *was* a reason her mother was smiling to herself: Besides wanting her daughter to be happy, her mother had also just eaten a large piece of fudge shaped like a canoe. But that didn't seem to be the time to admit something like that.

Thirteen

Did Amelia Earhart fly again the next day?

Why, yes she did.

And the day after that.

And the day after that.

And the day after that.

And every day for forty-nine days, other than day seven (when it rained), day nineteen (when she had to get a haircut), and day forty- four (when Dr. Young forgot that he'd given away the plane and took it for a drive across town at the precise moment he should have been in his office removing Mrs. Goldberg's wisdom teeth).

You probably think that by flying so

often, Amelia would have attracted a lot of attention. But really, back in those days, it was very, very rare to see things other than birds soaring in the sky—so people hardly ever looked up. *No one noticed Amelia's almost-daily flights.* Not her mother. Not Nelson Nelson. Not her next-door neighbor Franklin David Peppermouth. Not the man in the blue raincoat or his binocularless duck. Not anyone.

So it was with great excitement that Amelia studied her flight logbook and noticed that her next flight would be her 50th.

"Clearly, this has to be a special flight," the young lady told herself. So she walked, yes walked, to Horowitz's Maps, and bought the second-biggest map Horowitz had in the store (she'd wanted the biggest, but a magician had gotten there a few moments before and bought that one).

Then she took the map to Derek's Big, Thick Writing Tools Shop and bought the second biggest and thickest pen that Derek had in the store. (Again, the magician had gotten there first.)

Upon returning home, Amelia used those second-best tools to plot her 50th flight.

Amelia circled fifteen cities, four states, and eleven countries. Then she connected all the circles with lines, and...

Much to her surprise and delight...

IT MADE A KITTY CAT!

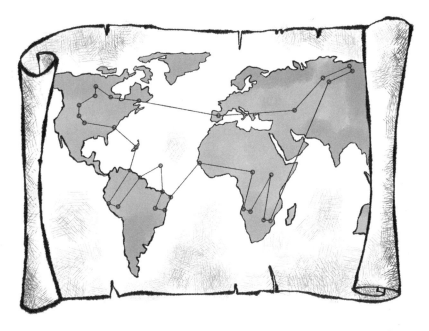

"Awww, that's so cute!" Amelia beamed, making a vow to hang that kitty-catted map on her wall right after she returned from her 50th flight.

"Eeney, Meenie, Miney, Shirley!" Amelia said to herself as she closed her eyes and tried to choose a destination at random. (Yes, these days, we say "Eeney, Meenie, Miney, Moe"—but that was many years before Moe was born and took over for Shirley.)

When Amelia opened her eyes again, she saw that, amazingly, her finger had landed on her own hometown! Incredible!

What's even more incredible is that she did the whole "Eeney, Meenie, Miney, Shirley!" thing three times more, and each time her finger ended up in the *exact same spot.*

Naturally, this was confusing and frustrating for the young aviator. So...she thought and thought and thought and thought, and finally decided to...use a different finger.

She also decided to keep one eye open to make sure she didn't end up picking the same destination. Though she couldn't decide which eye to keep open, so she did...

"Eeney, Meenie, Miney, Shirley!" until she picked her left eye as the one to stay open.

Then, she closed her right eye and said "Eeney, Meenie, Miney, Shirley!" again for the random picking. And when she opened her right eye, she saw that her finger was squarely on a place called Wagga Wagga, Australia.

Fourteen

Even with today's speedy jets (the airplane kind, not the football team kind), it takes a long time to fly from the United States to Australia. It certainly took even longer back when Amelia Earhart set her sights on Wagga Wagga.

Naturally, Amelia carefully packed for the lengthy journey. She brought potatoes, tomatoes, seventy-seven loaves of bread, a lollipop (cherry), and a slice of cheese (not Swiss, because she didn't like how the holes tasted).

She also packed quite a bit of clothing, including extra socks, shirts, pants, scarves,

gloves, and well, *you know what else* (hint: it starts with *u* and ends in *nderwear*).

"That ought to do it," she said to herself.

"Don't step one foot off our block!" her mother called from down the hall.

"I won't, mother!" Amelia responded. "I never do!" she added, knowing that she really wasn't planning to that day, and she really hadn't done so on any of her other trips.

"That's a good girl," her mother shouted. "And be home by seven!"

Amelia swallowed hard. It was 10:00 a.m. She knew that there was no way she'd ever make it to all the way there and back in nine hours—especially if she had to find a gas station while flying over the Pacific Ocean.

"Um, mom, I um, um," Amelia stumbled.

"That's a good girl," her mother shouted.

It was too much for Amelia to take. She walked down the hall and asked her mother to put down the brush and stop painting the suede couch for a moment.

"Mom," Amelia confessed. "I have something to tell you."

"Can I hear it, too?" her grandmother asked, entering the room on Amelia's grandfather's back.

"Me...oof, get off my back...too?" her grandfather asked as he placed Amelia's grandmother on the newly painted couch.

"After all, we've hardly been in the second half of this book *at all*," her grandmother added, not realizing that there was paint all over the back of her robe.

"And listen, I was mentioned on the first page of Chapter One, but there's been nothing about me since!" Amelia's father said as he climbed into the living room window.

Amelia took a deep breath and said, "I have a lot to tell you all. First, do you remember when I was little I always said I wanted to fly?"

"Yes," said her mother.

"I do," said her father.

"Indeed," said her grandfather.

"Why is there paint on the back of my robe?" said her grandmother.

"Well," Amelia continued. "I never gave up that dream. And I, I, well, I got an airplane and have flown it 49 times in all."

"Good joke," said her mother.

"Great joke," said her father.

"Best joke I've heard," said her grandfather.

"I mean it; why is there paint on the back

of my robe?" said her grandmother.

"I'm not kidding, Mom, Dad, Grandpapsy and Grandmamster," Amelia said. "I've been soaring up in the air almost every day for the past two months."

"I don't believe you," said her mother.

"I don't believe you either," said her father.

"I don't believe you either neither," said her grandfather.

"I don't believe I'm going to be able to remove this paint from the back of my robe," said her grandmother.

"Well it's all true! And today, I'm flying off to Wagga Wagga, Australia!"

"I'm sailing to Pittsburgh," laughed her mother.

"I'm swimming to Brooklyn," said her father.

"I'm tap-dancing to Utah," said her grandfather.

"I'm going to change into something without paint on it," said her grandmother.

"Well, it's too bad that no one believes me; I'll be going now," Amelia said. "Come outside and keep your eyes on the sky to watch me take off," she added.

Fifteen

Moments later, Amelia's mother, father, and grandfather all followed her to the backyard. They watched as Amelia put on her flying gear, hopped into V.O.M.I.T., checked her instruments, and ate the slice of cheese (for energy).

"Goodbyeeeeeeeeeeeeeeeeeee!" Amelia yelled as the plane started rolling for takeoff.

"What did she say?" her grandfather asked.

"Goodbyeeeeeeeeeeeeeeeee!" her father told him.

"No, it was 'Goodbyeeeeeeeeeeeeeeeeeee!' — with nineteen letter e's at the end," her mother said.

"I heard seventeen," said her father. "Goodbyeeeeeeeeeeeeeeeee!"

"Nope, I absolutely, definitely heard 'Goodbyeeeeeeeeeeeeeeeeeeee!'" her mother answered. "I'm sure of it."

"Well anyway, she's gone," said her grandfather.

"Why are all of you out here?" Amelia's grandmother asked as she joined the group, still wearing the paint-stained robe. "And where's Amelia?"

"She flew away," said Amelia's mom.

"To Australia," said Amelia's dad.

"Wagga Wagga," said Amelia's grandfather.

"Wagga Wagga to you too," laughed Amelia's grandmother. "Now c'mon, let's go in the house and wait for television to be invented."

And that's exactly what they did.

Sixteen

Did Amelia make it to Wagga Wagga? Did she enjoy the potatoes, tomatoes, and seventy-seven loaves of wheat bread? Did she wish she'd saved the slice of cheese for later in the flight?

These are all good questions.

And good questions deserve good answers. But like four-leaf clovers, pennies with cartoon characters on them, or two-year-old toddlers who are professional athletes, good answers are often hard to find.

Let's just say that the ending to this story is quite a bit like Amelia Earhart's life...

...up in the air!

Okay, now that you've read *The Lieography of Amelia Earhart*, you're probably wondering about the real life story of the great, great aviator.

Well, you're in luck; here are some factual facts about the pioneering woman. You can believe everything you're about to read, and it'd be great if you check out even more information about her.

Amelia Earhart was a terrific American aviator. She was born in Atchison, Kansas on July 24, 1897.

Amelia grew up with a strong interest in mechanical things—she even built her own roller coaster at age seven! For much of her childhood, she lived with her grandparents in Atchison during the winter, and with her parents in Kansas City in the summer (though they moved around a lot because of her father's work obligations, and she attended several different high schools).

Interestingly, it's said that Amelia had no particular interest in aviation during her childhood. But she did have an adventurous spirit, and she enjoyed participating in sports and other endeavors that were frowned upon for her, because they were considered more suitable for males back then.

Those attitudes (of course, unacceptable in today's society) didn't stop Amelia Earhart. She continually fought unfair stereotypes, blazing her own trail in her own way. And in doing so, she inspired countless other women and helped them turn their own ambitions and dreams into reality.

In 1918, Amelia became a nurse's aide in Canada, helping wounded soldiers who were coming home from World War I.

Amelia experienced her first flight at a California air show in December 1920. After that initial flight experience, she knew that she had to fly, and began taking flying lessons (which she paid for by working various office jobs). Not long after, she bought a bright yellow, pre-owned two-seater biplane that she named *The Canary*. It was in that plane that she became the first female to achieve a flying altitude of more than 14,000 feet.

A couple of years later, financial woes caused Amelia to sell *The Canary*. But she remained interested in flying, and got actively involved once again in 1927 (the year that Charles Lindbergh famously made a solo flight from New York to Paris).

A year later, Amelia was asked to be the first female to fly across the Atlantic. Though many considered it a risky expedition, Amelia bravely joined two male pilots for a 21-hour flight across the ocean from Newfoundland to Wales.

In 1932, the U.S. Congress awarded Amelia the Distinguished Flying Cross after she became the first female pilot to navigate the Atlantic in a solo journey (only Lindbergh had done it before her). That same year, she became the first woman to fly solo nonstop across the United States (her flight from Los Angeles to Newark, New Jersey took 19 hours).

Amelia's flights made her quite a popular figure. In addition to being known for her flying, she was a celebrated author, clothing designer, and aviation consultant at Purdue University.

In early July 1937, Amelia was determined to fly around the earth. She and a copilot took off on their journey...but due to fuel and radio communication problems, they were lost at sea. More than $4 million was spent on a rescue mission; sadly, that mission failed to locate the aviators or their aircraft.

It's been more than 80 years since her last flight, but Amelia Earhart remains a strong role model for those seeking courage and perseverance.

Author's Bio

Alan Katz has written more than 40 highly acclaimed children's books, including *Take Me Out of the Bathtub and Other Silly Dilly Songs*, *The Day the Mustache Took Over*, *OOPS!*, *Don't Say That Word!*, *Really Stupid Stories for Really Smart Kids*, and two *Awesome Achievers* titles. Alan has received many state awards for children's literature, and he frequently speaks at literacy conferences and schools around the country.

Alan is also a six-time Emmy-nominated writer for series including *The Rosie O'Donnell Show*, *Taz-Mania*, *Pinkalicious and Peterrific*, numerous Nickelodeon shows, and more. He hosted a long-running game show on SiriusXM's Kids Place Live channel, and he's also created comic books, trading cards, theme park shows, and hundreds of other special projects for kids and their parents.

Illustrator's Bio

Tracy Hill has been working as an illustrator since 1989, creating humorous and whimsical illustrations for clients in the advertising, editorial, and publishing fields. His true passion has been in illustrating children's books.

THANKS FOR READING
The Lieography of Amelia Earhart.

Also pick up other Lieographies:

The Lieography of Thomas Edison

The Lieography of Babe Ruth